Entrepreneurship

Navigating the Journey of Starting
and Growing a Business

Isaac Wilson

Table of Contents

Entrepreneurship

Entrepreneurship

Introduction

The idea of entrepreneurship is dynamic and multidimensional, embodying the spirit of business, risk-taking, and invention. In the quickly changing global environment of today, entrepreneurship is essential for stimulating economic growth, encouraging innovation, and providing chances for people to follow their passions and fulfill their aspirations. This section attempts to give a thorough introduction to entrepreneurship, including its definition, reasons to become an entrepreneur, and essential traits that lead to successful business.

Defining Entrepreneurship

Fundamentally, entrepreneurship is the process of spotting, generating, and seizing chances to launch new goods, services, or companies. To bring novel ideas to market, it entails managing obstacles, utilizing resources, and taking measured risks. Although the word "entrepreneurship" is frequently linked to launching a new business, it also refers to an entrepreneurial way of thinking and solving problems that may be used in a variety of contexts, including existing businesses.

Entrepreneurship encompasses a broad range of domains, including technology, healthcare, finance, hospitality, and more. It is not restricted to any one business or sector. While the backgrounds, experiences, and goals of entrepreneurs may differ, they are all driven to create value, challenge the status quo, and have a significant impact on the world.

Why Become an Entrepreneur

The choice to start a business is a very personal one that is impacted by many different things. For some people, becoming an entrepreneur allows them to break free from the confines of regular work, follow their passions, and realize their own vision. Some people are driven by the need to address unmet needs, find solutions to urgent societal issues, or take advantage of new trends and business opportunities.

Through successful companies that offer options for long-term growth and prosperity as well as considerable returns on investment, entrepreneurship also offers the chance to build wealth and financial freedom.

The possibility of creating a long-term legacy, influencing the course of history, and making a lasting impression on the globe via their creative endeavors and ideas also inspires a lot of entrepreneurs.

Characteristics of Successful Entrepreneurs

Even while creativity, desire, and resiliency are frequently linked to entrepreneurship, successful entrepreneurs have a variety of other qualities that add to their efficacy and influence. Among them are:

1. Vision and Passion: Entrepreneurs that are successful have a strong sense of what they want to accomplish and are extremely passionate about their objectives. Their fervor and dedication inspire them to surmount challenges, endure hardships, and maintain concentration on their ultimate goals.

2. Innovative Thinking: Creative problem-solving, questioning the status quo, and unconventional thinking are all skills that entrepreneurs possess. They never stop

looking for ways to innovate, disrupt, and better things, and they don't mind taking calculated chances to follow their ideas.

3. Resilience and Persistence: Establishing a profitable company is rarely an easy or straight path. Entrepreneurs need to have the fortitude to keep moving forward in the face of difficulties and setbacks as well as the resilience to reject offers and rejections. They see failures as teaching moments, chances for personal development, and stepping stones to future achievement.

4. Adaptability and Flexibility: The business environment is ever-changing due to the influence of emerging technology, market trends, and competitive pressures. Entrepreneurs who are successful are

adaptive and flexible; they can quickly change course in reaction to evolving situations, grab hold of fresh chances, and modify their approach as necessary to stay on top of the game.

5. Risk-Taking and Decision-Making: Risk, uncertainty, and ambiguity are a part of entrepreneurship by nature. Entrepreneurs that are successful are at ease with taking calculated chances, coming to difficult conclusions, and accepting uncertainty as a necessary component of the business journey. They acquire pertinent data, balance potential benefits against risks, and use intuition and thorough analysis to make well-informed decisions.

6. Strong Work Ethic and Discipline: Dedication, diligence, and discipline are necessary for creating a successful company. Entrepreneurs are prepared to invest the time, energy, and effort necessary to realize their ideas; they frequently put in long workdays and make sacrifices in order to achieve their objectives. They prioritize work well, hold themselves and their teams to high standards, and are unwaveringly focused on results and execution.

Entrepreneurship is a collaborative endeavor that necessitates entrepreneurs to interact with stakeholders, inspire confidence, and cultivate relationships with consumers, investors, employees, and other essential partners. This requires effective communication and leadership skills. Strong interpersonal and communication skills are a hallmark of successful entrepreneurs. These abilities include the capacity to clearly express their vision, persuade others, and inspire teams to accomplish common goals.

In conclusion, entrepreneurship attracts people from many walks of life who share the ambition to innovate, create value, and have a positive impact on the world. It offers a wide range of opportunities, challenges, and rewards. Aspiring entrepreneurs can start their own businesses with clarity, purpose, and confidence if they comprehend the concept of entrepreneurship, the reasons behind starting one, and the essential traits of successful entrepreneurs.

Chapter 1: Getting Started

Setting off on an entrepreneurial journey demands forethought, preparation, and a thorough comprehension of one's purpose, passion, and the state of the market. We go over the crucial first steps in this section, which include figuring out your purpose and passion, researching the market, and creating a business plan.

Identifying Your Purpose and Passion

Every prosperous business endeavor is driven by a deep-seated passion and sense of purpose. It's important to take stock of your hobbies, skills, values, and goals before venturing into the field of entrepreneurship in order to determine what genuinely inspires and motivates you. Pose challenging queries to yourself, such as:

- Which activities are my favorites?
- What issues or difficulties do I have a strong desire to resolve?
- What kind of influence do I hope to have on the world?
- What ideals do I want my company to uphold?

You can boost your chances of success and get more joy and happiness from your entrepreneurial pursuits by coordinating your business venture with your passions and purpose. Passion drives tenacity, inventiveness, and resilience, empowering you to conquer challenges and confidently ride out the ups and downs of entrepreneurship.

Performing Market Analysis

After determining your goal and area of passion, the following stage is to carry out in-depth market research to evaluate the viability and feasibility of your business idea. Obtaining and evaluating information about your target market, market trends, the competitive environment, and consumer demands and preferences is known as market research. Gaining insightful knowledge that supports strategic decision-making and puts your company in a successful position is the aim.

Important facets of market research consist of:

1. Target Market Analysis: Determine the characteristics, behaviors, psychographics, and pain points of your target clientele. Recognize their requirements, preferences, and buying patterns to customize your offerings.

2. Industry Analysis: Assess your industry's or niche market's size, development potential, and dynamics. Recognize new trends, developments in technology, modifications to laws and regulations, and

other elements that could affect the expansion and success of your company.

3. Competitor Analysis: Examine the advantages, disadvantages, tactics, and positioning of your rivals in the market. Find the gaps, the possibilities, and the places where you can set yourself apart from the competition with your services.

4. SWOT study: Evaluate the internal and external strengths and weaknesses of your company by doing a thorough SWOT (Strengths, Weaknesses, Opportunities, Threats) study. Utilize this research to pinpoint areas in need of development, reduce risks, and seize opportunities.

You can make well-informed decisions, reduce risks, and set up your company for long-term success in a cutthroat industry by arming yourself with practical market insights.

Creating a Business Idea

Now that you have a firm grasp on your passion, mission, and the state of the market, it's time to create a winning business concept that fills gaps in the market, solves issues, or satisfies demands in a novel and creative way.

The following steps will help you through the process:

1. Determine Your Niche: Concentrate on a certain target market or niche where you can stand out from the competition and provide value. Think of untapped markets or neglected niches in your sector where you can establish a unique competitive advantage.

2. Validate Your Idea: To get input, confirm presumptions, and gauge market demand, test your company idea with prospective clients, industry insiders, mentors, and advisers. Utilize focus groups, questionnaires, interviews, and prototype testing to get feedback and improve your idea.

3. Describe Your Value Proposition in Detail: Clearly state your company's

distinctive value proposition, which is what makes you stand out from the competition and convinces buyers to pick your goods or services. Determine which features, benefits, and value drivers are most appealing to your target market.

4. Build a Business Plan: Construct a thorough business plan that details your target market, value proposition, revenue streams, marketing approach, operating schedule, and projected financials. An effective business plan acts as a road map for your endeavor, assisting with decision-making, drawing in investors, and obtaining funding.

5. Initiate Little and Continue: Start with a prototype or minimal viable product (MVP),

and iterate in response to user feedback and market validation. To maximize performance and scalability, test and improve your distribution channels, messaging, pricing, and offerings.

These methods will help you focus on a workable business idea that will fit your passion, mission, and market opportunity. Once you have this, you can build a strong foundation for an entrepreneurial endeavor that will hopefully succeed and have a significant impact.

With the help of this chapter, prospective business owners can gain useful insights and helpful advice for beginning their venture. Creating a strong company idea, researching the industry, and discovering interests are all critical steps in preparing yourself for success in the fast-paced, cutthroat world of entrepreneurship.

Chapter 2: Business Planning

A new venture's potential to succeed and last is largely dependent on its ability to plan its business. To fuel growth and inform decision-making, it entails meticulously creating a roadmap for your company that outlines important strategies, objectives, and operational specifics. We'll go over the key elements of company planning in this section, such as drafting a business plan, establishing goals and objectives, and comprehending legal and regulatory requirements.

Developing a Business Plan

A business plan is an all-inclusive document that describes the objectives, strategies, goals, vision, and operational specifics of a company. It offers a path for business owners to take, assisting them in overcoming obstacles, grabbing chances, and achieving sustained success. A business strategy should have the following essential components:

1. Executive Summary: Provides a succinct synopsis of the company, outlining its value proposition, target market, competitive advantage, mission, and financial highlights.

2. Business Description: Comprehensive details regarding the type of business, its goods and services, the target market's composition, a study of the industry, and the competitive environment.

3. Market analysis: Comprehensive investigation and evaluation of the target market, consumer demands and inclinations, market trends, rival assessment, and market division.

4. Marketing and Sales Strategy: A well-thought-out plan that contains distribution networks, price strategies, marketing channels, promotional strategies, and sales predictions in order to reach and acquire customers.

5.   Operations and Management: Information regarding the production or service delivery process, important personnel, operational procedures, organizational structure, and management team duties.

6. Financial Plan: Comprises projections of income, expenses, cash flow, and profitability for a certain period, along with balance sheets, cash flow statements, and income statements. covers financial assumptions, capital sources, and finance requirements as well.

7. Risk Management Plan: A plan for identifying, evaluating, and mitigating possible risks and challenges to the organization in order to reduce their impact.

It takes thorough investigation, analysis, and strategic planning to create a comprehensive company plan. For entrepreneurs, it acts as a road map, assisting in decision-making, drawing in investors, obtaining funding, and guaranteeing the long-term viability and prosperity of the company.

Setting Objectives and Goals

A business's direction and success must be guided by the establishment of specific, attainable goals and objectives. Objectives set precise, quantifiable targets for accomplishing goals, whereas goals give a sense of direction and purpose. Here's how to make goals and objectives work for you:

1. Vision and Mission: Establish the overarching goals and objectives of the company, which are what give it its ultimate purpose and inspire it to exist.

2. SMART Goals: Assign SMART (specific, measurable, attainable, relevant, and time-bound) goals to yourself. This guarantees responsibility, lucidity, and congruence with the overarching corporate plan.

3. Short- and Long-Term Objectives: Divide your objectives into short-term (quarterly or annual) and long-term (three to five years) segments. Long-term objectives establish

the course for future development and success, whilst short-term objectives offer immediate concentration and direction.

4. KPIs (Key Performance Indicators): Define particular KPIs to monitor performance in relation to goals and objectives and gauge progress. Sales goals, KPIs related to acquiring customers, profitability margins, and operational efficiency measures are a few examples.

5. Regular Review and Adjustment: Track goals' progress over time, evaluate results in relation to KPIs, and make necessary modifications to stay on course and adjust for shifting market conditions.

Establishing definite, achievable goals and targets enables business owners to concentrate their energies, assign work in a timely manner, and evaluate their progress efficiently. Entrepreneurs can guarantee responsibility, stimulate performance, and accomplish sustainable growth and success by coordinating goals with the overarching business plan and keeping a close eye on advancements.

Understanding Legal and Regulatory Needs

A crucial part of launching and running a business is navigating the legal and regulatory environment. Financial penalties, reputational harm, and legal repercussions may arise from breaking applicable rules and regulations. Here is a summary of the main legal and regulatory issues that entrepreneurs should be aware of:

1. Business Structure: Select a limited liability company (LLC), corporation, partnership, or sole proprietorship as the legal form for your organization. The effects on ownership, taxation, responsibility, and governance vary depending on the structure.

2. Licensing and firm Registration: Obtain the licenses and permissions required to operate lawfully in your jurisdiction, and register your firm with the relevant government authorities. Requirements change based on the industry, region, kind of business, and other variables.

3. Intellectual Property Protection: Preserve your brand, inventions, and creative works from unapproved use or infringement by protecting your intellectual property (IP) assets, such as patents, trade secrets, copyrights, and trademarks.

4. Taxation and Compliance: Recognize your responsibility for paying income taxes, sales taxes, payroll taxes, and other local, state, and federal taxes. To guarantee compliance and reduce tax obligations, speak with an accountant or tax counselor.

5. Employment Laws and Regulations: Learn about the rules and laws pertaining to hiring, pay, benefits, overtime, harassment, and other labor-related matters. To safeguard your staff and reduce legal risks,

make sure employment regulations are followed.

6. Agreements and Contracts: To safeguard your rights and set explicit terms and conditions for partnerships, business transactions, leases, and other arrangements, carefully draft and negotiate agreements, contracts, and other legal documents.

7. Data Privacy and Security: Put in place safeguards against cyber risks, illegal access, and breaches for sensitive data, customer information, and private company records. Respect regulations pertaining to data privacy, such as the Health Insurance Portability and Accountability Act (HIPAA)

in the US and the General Data Protection Regulation (GDPR) in Europe.

Entrepreneurs may find it difficult to navigate the legal and regulatory requirements, but doing so is necessary to assure compliance, reduce risks, and safeguard the integrity and reputation of the company. To address particular legal difficulties and make sure that applicable laws and regulations are followed, seek professional legal advice and guidance.

Entrepreneurs can reduce risks, build a strong foundation for their businesses, and raise the possibility of long-term success and sustainability by developing thorough business plans, setting SMART goals and targets, and being aware of the legal and regulatory environment. In order to promote growth, ensure legal and regulatory compliance, and direct decision-making, each component is essential.

Chapter 3: Financing Your Business

Getting funding is an essential first step in starting and expanding a business. The success and longevity of your business can be greatly impacted by knowing the different financing choices available and selecting the appropriate funding sources, regardless of whether you're a startup or seasoned business owner trying to expand. This section will cover the various ways to finance your business, such as funding sources, pitching to investors, and bootstrapping vs. seeking investment.

Seeking Funding vs. Bootstrapping

The term "bootstrapping" describes the process of financing your own company out of personal savings, sales proceeds, or other available resources. Through bootstrapping, business owners can keep total control and ownership of their company, prevent stock and debt dilution, and preserve their decision-making freedom and autonomy.

However, because resources are usually limited and growth may be slower than in enterprises with external investment, bootstrapping may limit the scale and growth potential of your business.

Seeking outside funding, on the other hand, entails raising money from lenders, investors, or other sources in order to support growth, expansion, or operational activities for the company. Access to more money, knowledge, and resources is made possible by external investment, which can be used to expand operations, speed up growth, and seize opportunities. It does, however, frequently include giving up equity or taking on debt, as well as significant risks and duties like shareholder agreements, investor expectations, and payback requirements.

The choice of whether to seek finance or bootstrap your firm is influenced by a number of factors, such as your access to capital, risk tolerance, growth targets, and business nature. Many entrepreneurs choose to combine the two strategies, using the money they bootstrapped to prove their idea, gain traction, and draw in outside lenders or investors for additional development and expansion.

Types of Funding Sources

Entrepreneurs have access to a variety of funding sources, each with unique benefits, prerequisites, and factors to take into account. Typical financing sources include the following:

1. Bootstrapping: Financing business operations and expansion with credit card debt, personal savings, or sales proceeds.

Bootstrapping enables business owners to keep total control and ownership over their enterprise, but it may limit potential for growth and necessitate careful money management.

2. Loans: Taking out loans to finance business ventures from banks, credit unions, or other lenders. Loans can be classified as unsecured (based on creditworthiness) or secured (backed by collateral), and they usually include an interest-bearing repayment period. Term loans, credit lines, and Small Business Administration (SBA) loans are common forms of business lending.

3. Investors: Obtaining funds in return for equity ownership or a share in the company

from institutional investors, private equity firms, angel investors, and venture capitalists. To assist entrepreneurs in expanding and growing their companies, investors offer capital, knowledge, and strategic advice. Presenting a strong company strategy, financial estimates, and growth prospects to investors is part of the pitching process.

4. Crowdfunding: Obtaining funds via a large number of backers or individual investors via internet platforms like Indiegogo, Kickstarter, or GoFundMe. Without giving up equity or taking on debt, crowdfunding enables business owners to validate their concept, create pre-sales, and raise money from a wide range of supporters. To draw donors and meet

financial targets, though, successful marketing, promotion, and engagement are needed.

5. Grants and Awards: Getting non-dilutive funds via grants, contests, or awards from governmental bodies, charitable institutions, or corporate sponsors. Grants and awards, which usually don't require repayment or equity involvement, provide money for particular projects, research endeavors, or social impact endeavors.

Every financing source has its own requirements for eligibility, application procedure, and pros and downsides. Entrepreneurs ought to thoroughly examine the funding options available to them, weigh the advantages and disadvantages of each one, and select the best sources for their particular set of goals, stage of development, and risk tolerance.

Making a pitch to investors

Making a pitch to potential investors is a vital first step in getting outside investment for your company. A strong pitch might mean the difference between getting funding or not, whether you're presenting to venture capitalists, angel investors, or other funding sources.

The following are some essential pointers for creating and presenting a compelling investment pitch:

1. Craft an Engaging Story: Begin with a succinct and straightforward story that emphasizes the issue you're trying to solve, the market potential, and your special selling point. Tell a captivating story to investors to pique their interest and generate enthusiasm for your venture.

2. Emphasize Progress and Turning Points: Highlight your most significant successes, traction, and milestones to date, including partnerships, awards, revenue growth, customer acquisition, and product development. Give investors proof of market validation and advancement to reassure them.

3. Make a compelling value Proposition: Clearly state your company's value

proposition, which is what makes you stand out from the competition and convinces buyers to pick your goods or services. Emphasize the characteristics, advantages, and points of uniqueness that your offering offers that will appeal to and convince your target market.

4. Showcase the Market Potential: Give information and analysis regarding the target market's size, potential for growth, and characteristics. Present data demonstrating the unmet needs, client pain areas, and market demand that your company is trying to meet. To bolster your arguments, include market data, client endorsements, and a competition analysis.

5. Explain the Financials and Business Model: Describe the processes your company uses to bring in money, attract clients, and turn a profit. Provide a comprehensible, expandable company plan that exhibits long-term viability and expansion possibilities. To show the financial sustainability of your company, provide financial projections that include cash flow forecasts, spending breakdowns, and revenue estimates.

6. Address Risks and obstacles: To reassure investors and show that you are prepared, acknowledge potential risks, obstacles, and mitigation strategies.

7. Involve and Connect: Build a relationship with investors by having meaningful

conversations with them, posing inquiries, and paying attention to their opinions and worries. Be really passionate, enthusiastic, and confident in your company's ability to succeed.

8. Offer a Well-Received Presentation: Make a polished, eye-catching pitch deck to go along with your spoken presentation. To effectively communicate your idea, use storytelling tactics, clear, succinct language, and eye-catching images. To make sure your pitch is clear, coherent, and delivered with confidence, practice it several times.

9. Act Authentically and Transparently: Be open and honest about your company's advantages, disadvantages, opportunities, and threats. In your dealings with investors,

be truthful, sincere, and transparent while addressing any possible worries or uncertainties.

10. Follow Up and Stay Engaged: Following the pitch meeting, get in touch with investors as soon as possible to address any concerns, offer further details, and give them an update on your project. Throughout the fundraising process, remain in touch and connect with investors on a frequent basis to establish rapport and trust.

Careful planning, gripping storytelling, and proficient communication are necessary when making a pitch to potential investors. Through the creation of an engaging pitch that emphasizes your company's distinct selling point, market potential, momentum, and financial sustainability, you may draw in investors, obtain capital, and take your company to new heights of achievement.

One of the most important parts of being an entrepreneur is getting your firm funded. Navigating the process of launching and expanding a profitable endeavor requires knowing the different funding alternatives that are accessible.

Giving your financial demands, objectives, and available resources considerable thought is essential, regardless of whether you decide to pursue a combination of both ways, bootstrap, or look for outside assistance. You may fulfill your entrepreneurial vision and accomplish your business goals by looking into various funding options, making a strong pitch to investors, and obtaining the money required to support the expansion and success of your company.

Chapter 4: Building Your Brand

Developing a strong brand is crucial to setting your company apart from the competition, drawing clients, and encouraging trust and loyalty. To stand out and achieve success in the cutthroat industry of today, you must develop a unique brand identity and communicate your value proposition clearly. We'll go over important topics related to developing your brand in this area, such as creating a distinctive value proposition, branding tactics, and marketing and promotion methods.

Developing Your Unique Value Proposition

The essence of your brand is your unique value proposition (UVP), which explains what makes your company different from the competition and why buyers should select your goods or services. It takes in-depth knowledge of your target market, client wants and preferences, and the competitive landscape to create an engaging UVP. The following actions will assist you in identifying and expressing your UVP:

1. Identify Customer Needs: Find out what the needs, wants, and motivations of your target market are by conducting market research. Determine any unmet needs,

difficulties, or market gaps that your company can fill.

2. Highlight Differentiators: Determine the special qualities, benefits, and strengths that set your company apart from rivals. This could involve elements like the quality, price, customer service, and personality of the brand or the qualities of the product.

3. Showcase Benefits: Clearly outline the advantages and worth that your goods and services provide to clients. Pay attention to how your products or services improve the lives of your target market, solve issues, or satisfy requirements.

4. Be Clear and Concise: Condense your UVP into a few words or sentences that are

memorable and succinct. Use straightforward language that is understandable to your target audience instead of jargon or technical terms.

5. Test and Iterate: To confirm your UVP and make sure it appeals to your target audience, gather input from clients, associates, and industry experts. Refine and iterate your messaging in response to feedback and insights to keep raising your UVP.

All facets of your marketing and communication initiatives are directed by a robust UVP, which forms the cornerstone of your brand identity and messaging. It enables you to establish a connection with your target market, set yourself apart from rivals, and provide clients a strong reason to choose your brand.

Strategies for Branding

A logo or visual identity is merely one aspect of branding; branding is the whole consumer experience, from the first point of contact to continued connections and interactions. With your target audience, effective branding techniques help create feelings, mold perceptions, and foster loyalty and trust. The following are important branding tactics to think about:

1. Define Your Brand Identity: Create a distinct and unified brand identity that captures your essence, character, and

market positioning. This covers components like your logo, colors, font, graphics, voice, and imagery for your brand.

2. Consistency is Key: Make sure that your website, social media accounts, marketing materials, packaging, and consumer interactions are all consistent across all brand touchpoints and platforms. Maintaining consistency in your branding helps clients recognize and trust your business.

3. Tell Your Story: To interact and establish a deeper connection with your audience, use storytelling. Talk about your brand's origins, goals, core principles, and the path that led to your goods and services. Genuine

storytelling forges emotional bonds with consumers and humanizes your brand.

4. Create company connections: By continuously upholding your company's values and promise, you can build powerful brand connections. Encourage gratifying interactions and connections with clients to increase brand advocacy and loyalty.

5. Differentiate Your Brand: Set yourself apart from the competition by emphasizing your advantages, such as cutting-edge items, first-rate customer support, or an engaging brand narrative. To stand out in the market, concentrate on your advantages over the competition.

6. Engage Your Audience: Use events, content marketing, social media, and other platforms to encourage engagement and conversation with your audience. Promote user-generated material, comments, and involvement to build a feeling of community and identity around your business.

7. Monitor and Adapt: To evaluate the success of your branding strategy, keep an eye on market trends, consumer input, and brand performance. To remain current and resonate with your target audience, adjust and improve your strategy as necessary.

By putting these branding tactics into practice, you can develop a powerful and enduring brand identity that connects with your target market, fosters customer loyalty and trust, and propels your company's long-term success.

Promotion and Marketing Strategies

Using efficient marketing and promotion strategies is crucial to growing your company's brand recognition, customer base, and revenue. A well-executed marketing plan aids in reaching your target audience, communicating your value proposition, and generating interest and engagement whether you use digital marketing or traditional advertising. The following are important marketing and promotion strategies to think about:

1. Digital Marketing: To reach and interact with your target audience, use digital channels including websites, social media, email marketing, search engine optimization (SEO), and online advertising. Establish a powerful online presence, produce insightful content, and employ focused messaging to draw in prospects and turn them into clients. Use tactics like email newsletters, pay-per-click (PPC) campaigns, social media advertising, content marketing, and pay-per-click (PPC) campaigns to increase website traffic, lead generation, and audience engagement.

2. Content Marketing: Produce pertinent, high-quality content that enlightens, amuses, or motivates your target audience. Create a variety of content types, including

blog posts, articles, videos, infographics, podcasts, and case studies, as part of a content strategy that is in line with your brand's values and messaging. Optimize your content for search engines to boost discoverability and reach, and share it on other platforms to boost exposure and engagement.

3. Social Media Marketing: Interact with your followers on Facebook, Instagram, Twitter, LinkedIn, and Pinterest, among other social media sites. Create a social media plan that emphasizes establishing connections, disseminating insightful information, and encouraging community involvement. Utilize tools and analytics to analyze the effectiveness of your social

media activities, track performance, and keep an eye on conversations.

4. Email Marketing: Use email marketing campaigns to cultivate a relationship with your audience. To offer pertinent and customized material, segment your email list according to demographics, interests, or purchasing patterns. Then, tailor your messaging. Email automation can help you deliver automatic messages depending on user activities, optimize campaigns for higher engagement and conversion rates, and streamline procedures.

5. Search Engine Optimization (SEO): Use SEO strategies to raise your website's exposure and position in search engine results pages (SERPs). Enhance the

structure, content, and metadata of your website with pertinent terms and phrases, and establish high-quality backlinks from reliable websites. Make sure your website is always up to date, audited, and compliant with search engine algorithms so that users have a positive experience.

6. Online Advertising: To expand reach and visibility, pair your organic marketing activities with online advertising initiatives. Use platforms like sponsored content, Facebook ads, LinkedIn ads, and Google Ads to market your goods and services, reach a targeted audience, and increase traffic to your website or landing pages. To optimize return on investment (ROI) and meet your advertising goals, track the effectiveness of your ads, modify the

targeting criteria, and improve the ad creative.

7. Classic Advertising: To reach a wider audience and increase brand exposure, look into classic advertising channels including print, radio, television, outdoor billboards, and direct mail. Create imaginative and captivating advertising campaigns that speak to your target audience and complement the messaging and core values of your brand. Utilize response rates, brand recall, and audience reach to gauge the success of your traditional advertising campaigns.

8. Public Relations (PR): To secure media attention and improve the reputation of your brand, cultivate a good rapport with

influencers, media outlets, and industry stakeholders. Create a public relations plan that emphasizes thought leadership, storytelling, and community involvement. Then, send journalists and bloggers links to pertinent articles, stories, or events. Track sentiment, keep an eye on media mentions, and take proactive measures to manage the public perception and reputation of your brand.

9. Event Marketing: To meet your target audience face-to-face and present your goods or services, host or support conferences, workshops, webinars, or other events. Engage in industry trade shows, exhibitions, or networking gatherings to broaden your audience, cultivate connections, and produce leads. Make the

most of events to interact with guests, get their input, and learn about their preferences and industry trends.

10. Word-of-Mouth and Referral Marketing: Use word-of-mouth and referral marketing to get happy consumers to tell others about their excellent experiences and suggest your brand. To encourage customer advocacy and promote referrals, create incentive schemes, loyalty rewards programs, or referral programs. Building brand advocates and fostering strong customer connections requires going above and beyond what is expected of you in order to create natural word-of-mouth advertising.

You may boost business development and profitability, draw in and keep consumers, and raise brand awareness by putting these marketing and promotion strategies into practice. Try out various tactics, monitor performance indicators, and modify your strategy in response to feedback and insights to maximize your marketing efforts and meet your company goals.

Chapter 5: Launching Your Business

An exciting and crucial step in your entrepreneurial journey is launching your business. It represents the end of months or even years of diligent planning, hard labor, and preparation. We'll go over the crucial processes for starting a firm in this section, such as organizing operations, assembling your staff, and handling money and resources.

Setting up Operations

Setting up operations entails creating the fundamental systems and procedures required to manage your company profitably and successfully. Consider the following important steps:

1. Select Your Business Structure: Choose a legal form, such as a corporation, limited liability company (LLC), partnership, or sole proprietorship, based on your organization's needs and objectives. When selecting your business structure, take into account elements like liability protection, tax ramifications, and regulatory needs.

2. Register Your Business: Get any licenses or permits required to operate lawfully in your jurisdiction, and register your business name with the relevant government authorities. You might have to register for business licenses or permissions from the

federal, state/provincial, and municipal governments, depending on your industry and place of business.

3. Set Up Financial Accounts: To keep your personal and business finances apart, open business bank accounts, such as checking and savings accounts. Create merchant accounts to receive payments from clients, and install accounting programs or other tools to monitor earnings, outlays, and money exchanges.

4. Secure Physical or Virtual Space: If necessary, secure a physical site for your company, such as an office, manufacturing plant, or storefront. As an alternative, set up a remote workspace or virtual office to carry out business transactions online. When

selecting your office, take into account elements like location, ease of access, lease terms, and infrastructure requirements.

5. Invest in Technology and Equipment: Get or rent the tools, equipment, and technology you need to support your company's activities. Depending on your business and industry, this could be computers, software, machinery, cars, or other specialized equipment. Invest in dependable, expandable solutions that will satisfy your demands today and foster growth in the future.

6. Create Supply Chain and Logistics: Find and build connections with vendors, partners, and suppliers to acquire products, services, or raw materials for your company.

Create effective supply chain and logistics procedures to control inventories, complete orders, and provide clients with goods or services on time.

7. Implement Operational Processes: To simplify and standardize your company's processes, create workflows and standard operating procedures (SOPs). In order to guarantee uniformity, responsibility, and effectiveness throughout your company, clearly define roles and duties, create lines of communication, and record important procedures.

Building Your Team

Developing a solid and well-coordinated workforce is crucial to your company's success. assemble a bright, driven group of people that are committed to the same goals and beliefs as you. Here's how to properly assemble your team:

1. Define Roles and Responsibilities: Clearly state what each position in your company is expected to do as well as its roles. Determine the abilities, credentials, and work history needed for each position, then create job descriptions that will draw in eligible applicants.

2. Recruit Top Talent: Find and select competent applicants who fit your company's culture and have the know-how and experience required to be successful in

their positions. To draw in top talent, use a variety of recruitment channels, including job boards, social media, networking gatherings, and employee recommendations.

3. Promote Diversity and Inclusion: Create an inclusive and varied workplace that honors and embraces the variety of people's experiences, viewpoints, and backgrounds. Encourage diversity and inclusion policies, programs, and activities to make the workplace a friendly and encouraging place for all workers.

4. Offer Training and Development: Make an investment in courses that will improve the abilities, know-how, and skills of your team members. Provide chances for career

promotion, professional development, and ongoing learning to empower staff members and promote organizational success.

5. Promote Communication and Collaboration: Motivate your team members to communicate honestly, cooperate with one another, and work as a team. Set up regular brainstorming sessions, feedback channels, and meetings to promote communication, exchange ideas, and successfully handle obstacles.

6. Empower and Delegate: Give your team members the freedom to own their work and decide for themselves within their purview. Assign work and projects in accordance with each person's skills, interests, and personal

growth objectives. Offer assistance and direction when required.

7. Recognize and Reward Performance: To inspire and encourage your team members, recognize and honor outstanding work, contributions, and accomplishments. Put in place programs for employee appreciation and awards, such as bonuses, incentives, or events, to express gratitude for their commitment and hard work.

You may take advantage of different viewpoints and skill sets, encourage innovation and creativity, and accomplish your business objectives more successfully by assembling a bright and driven team.

Financial and Resource Management

Effective resource and financial management is essential to the long-term viability and expansion of your company. Here are some crucial methods for effectively allocating resources and handling finances:

1. Make a Budget: For the next few months or years, create a detailed budget that details your expected revenue, expenses, and cash flow. Ensure that resources are allocated in a way that maximizes returns on investment and gives priority to necessities while avoiding wasteful spending.

2. Monitor Cash Flow: Keep a close eye on your cash flow to keep tabs on your inflow of funds, outflow of expenses, and levels of liquidity. Keep enough cash on hand to pay for unforeseen emergencies, debt payments, and operating costs. To maximize cash flow efficiency, put cash flow management techniques into practice, such as sending out invoices on time, negotiating favorable conditions for payments, and controlling inventory levels.

3. management Costs: Reduce overhead, boost profitability, and optimize financial performance by putting cost management measures into place. Find areas where you can reduce costs, bargain with suppliers for better terms, and get rid of unnecessary spending. To find areas where costs might

be cut and to make necessary modifications, monitor and assess spending on a regular basis.

4. handle Debt appropriately: Create a plan to appropriately handle any outstanding debt and make gradual payments toward it. Give priority to loans with high interest rates, and look into options for consolidation or refinancing to cut interest rates and lower monthly payments. Steer clear of taking on too much debt or depending too much on credit to fund your company's operations.

5. Invest Wisely: To create long-term returns and value for your company, carefully consider investment opportunities and strategically distribute resources. When

choosing an investment, take into account variables including risk, ROI, and alignment with your company's goals. Spread out your assets to reduce risk and increase possible returns.

6. Keep an Eye on and Examine Financial Results: Monitor important financial data and performance indicators to evaluate the profitability and overall health of your company. To spot patterns, opportunities, and places for improvement, go over financial statements on a regular basis. These include the income statement, balance sheet, and cash flow statement. To make wise selections and modify your tactics as necessary to reach your financial objectives, do scenario planning and financial analysis.

7. Seek Professional assistance: For knowledgeable direction and assistance on handling your company's money, speak with financial experts, accountants, or business consultants. Utilize their knowledge to create long-term financial planning, risk reduction, tax planning, and financial management plans. Use their advice and insights to guide your decision-making and improve your financial success.

8. Implement Financial Controls: Set up internal policies and processes to protect your company's assets, stop fraud, and make sure that all financial rules and reporting requirements are followed. Put in place authorization procedures, monitoring systems, and job segregation to keep

financial processes transparent and accountable.

9. Get Ready for Emergencies: As you operate your business, you should anticipate and be ready for any financial difficulties, hiccups, or emergencies. Create emergency funds, contingency plans, and risk mitigation techniques to lessen the effects of unanticipated catastrophes like natural disasters, economic downturns, or changes in regulations.

10. analyze and Adjust: To assess your progress toward your objectives and pinpoint areas for improvement, periodically analyze your financial performance, budgets, and predictions. To evaluate performance versus goals and find

areas for optimization, do variance analysis, benchmarking, and financial modeling. To meet your financial goals and adjust to shifting market conditions, make the necessary adjustments to your plans, budgets, and strategies.

You can maximize profitability, reduce risk, and set up your company for long-term success by managing your finances and resources well.

You may overcome obstacles, take advantage of opportunities, and accomplish your long-term business objectives by putting good financial management techniques into practice and making well-informed decisions.

Starting a business is a complex process that needs to be planned carefully, strategically, and executed well. Establishing a strong foundation for your firm and positioning it for long-term success and growth may be achieved by hiring a skilled staff, setting up operations, and managing finances and resources effectively. In the face of obstacles and uncertainty as you set out on this thrilling adventure, remember to be adaptive, flexible, and resilient. You may achieve your goals of being a successful business owner and fulfilling your entrepreneurial aspirations with commitment, tenacity, and a well-defined vision.

Chapter 6: Navigating Challenges

A path of highs and lows, achievements and losses, awaits those who pursue entrepreneurship. A fundamental aspect of being an entrepreneur is overcoming obstacles. To thrive in the face of hardship, entrepreneurs need to cultivate resilience and adaptability, from overcoming rejection and failure to handling uncertainty and competition. This section will examine the main obstacles faced by entrepreneurs and the approaches that can be used to overcome them.

Getting Past Rejection and Failure

An unavoidable aspect of becoming an entrepreneur is failure. Failure is a typical event for entrepreneurs, whether it's a product launch that doesn't live up to expectations, an unsuccessful marketing campaign, or a business idea that doesn't take off. But in the end, your success may depend on how you handle defeat. Here are some methods for conquering rejection and failure:

1. See Failure as an Educational Experience: Consider failure as a worthwhile educational opportunity rather than a setback. Examine what went wrong, note the lessons that were learnt, and apply those conclusions to refine

and expand upon your strategy. Adopt a growth mindset that sees innovation and progress as coming from failure.

2. Remain Resilient and Persistent: Resilience is the capacity to overcome hardship and failures. Resilience can be developed through upholding a positive outlook, remaining committed to your long-term objectives, and persevering in the face of difficulties. When times are hard, don't give up and never forget that failures are only temporary roadblocks on the way to achievement.

3. Seek Feedback and Support: Seek input from peers, mentors, or customers to obtain insightful information about areas that require development. Don't be scared to ask

for comments. Embrace a network of mentors, advisors, and fellow entrepreneurs who can provide direction, inspiration, and insight when things go tough.

4. Adapt and Pivot: If your first plan doesn't produce the expected outcomes, be prepared to change course and modify your plan in light of customer feedback and industry developments. In order to determine what works best for your company, have an agile and adaptable mindset and be willing to try out new concepts and strategies.

5. Celebrate Small Wins: In spite of setbacks, acknowledge and honor minor triumphs and accomplishments along the path. Acknowledge and celebrate your

accomplishments, no matter how small, and use them as inspiration to keep going.

Dealing with Uncertainty and Risk

Being an entrepreneur is dangerous by nature; it's full of ambiguity, uncertainty, and unpredictability. In order to minimize risks and optimize possibilities, entrepreneurs need to develop their ability to handle ambiguity and successfully manage risk. Here are a few methods for handling risk and uncertainty:

1. Conduct Extensive Planning and Research: Before starting your company or taking on a new project, reduce uncertainty by performing in-depth competitive

analysis, market research, and feasibility studies. Compile information, gain understanding, and, using analysis and supporting data, make wise choices.

2. Craft Backup Strategies: To lessen the impact of any hazards on your company, prepare ahead of time and create backup plans. Develop proactive methods to counter potential hazards, such as shifts in market conditions, difficulties with regulations, or interruptions in the supply chain.

3. Diversify and Spread Risk: Broaden your clientele, revenue sources, and range of goods and services to reduce risk. Reducing your exposure to risk can be achieved by exploring chances to expand into new markets or verticals and avoiding an

over-reliance on a single source of income or a small number of clients.

4. Remain Adaptive and Agile: Survival in a business environment that is changing quickly requires flexibility and agility. Maintain your flexibility and responsiveness to changing consumer preferences, market dynamics, and new trends. To stay ahead of the curve, be ready to modify your approach, your services, or the way you allocate resources.

5. Manage Financial Risk: Prevent excessive debt or leverage, have healthy cash reserves, and regulate spending to manage financial risk. To guard against future financial losses, keep a careful eye on your financial performance and put risk management

techniques like insurance or hedging into practice.

Handling Competition and Changes in the Market

Entrepreneurs have to deal with intense competition and ongoing market shifts in today's extremely competitive business environment. Entrepreneurs need to create plans for handling rivalry and adjusting to the demands of the market if they want to prosper in this setting. The following advice will help you deal with market shifts and competition effectively:

1. Distinguish Your Offering: Make your goods or services stand out from those of

your rivals by emphasizing special qualities, advantages, or value propositions. To gain an edge over competitors and draw clients, concentrate on providing great quality, customer service, or innovation.

2. Remain Customer-Centric: Concentrate on comprehending the requirements, inclinations, and problems of your clients, then craft your services to effectively solve their demands and problems. To set your business apart from the competition, cultivate close bonds with your clients and give their happiness and loyalty top priority.

3. Keep an eye on rivals and Market trends: To remain up to date with market dynamics and industry trends, keep a careful watch on the actions, plans, and products of your

rivals. To determine your competitors' advantages, disadvantages, opportunities, and dangers, regularly analyze the competition. Then, utilize this information to guide your own strategy and decision-making.

4. Invent and Adapt: Keep your business strategy, services, and products innovative and ever-evolving to stay one step ahead of the competition. Encourage experimentation and innovation within your company, and keep an open mind when it comes to new concepts, tools, and fashions that can upend your sector or open up fresh avenues for expansion.

5. Put an emphasis on Value and Quality: Rather than competing on price or

undercutting rivals, concentrate on providing your clients with greater value and quality. In order to effectively reach your target audience, highlight the special advantages and benefits of your offerings. You may set yourself apart from the competition and develop a devoted following of customers who are less vulnerable to your competitors by offering outstanding value and quality.

6. Build Strategic Partnerships: Work together to take use of the knowledge, resources, and networks of suppliers, industry partners, and complementary firms. Creating mutually beneficial synergies, breaking into new markets, and broadening your reach are all possible with the aid of strategic alliances. Seek out

chances to work together on cooperative projects, co-marketing campaigns, or joint ventures that improve your competitive edge and promote growth for both parties.

7. Be Flexible and Responsive: Have the ability to quickly adjust to changes in the market or competitive environment. Keep your mind open to new possibilities and threats, and be prepared to modify your plan of action, your methods, or your priorities in order to remain competitive. To stay ahead of the curve, keep a careful eye on consumer preferences, market trends, and competition moves. Then, be prepared to adjust your strategy as necessary.

8. Invest in Continuous Improvement: To sustain a competitive advantage, it is

imperative to consistently assess and enhance your processes, products, and operations through "Investment in Continuous Improvement". To be at the forefront of your sector, make investments in R&D, innovative products, and process optimization. Get input from stakeholders, staff, and clients, and utilize it to inform continuous enhancements and modifications to your products.

In the face of shifting business dynamics and competitive pressures, entrepreneurs can position themselves for long-term success and resilience by using these tactics for managing competition and market changes. Entrepreneurs may succeed in even the most demanding and cutthroat business conditions by continuing to be customer-centric, inventive, and adaptive.

A crucial part of the entrepreneurial path is overcoming obstacles. Entrepreneurs may surmount challenges and prosper in the fast-paced, cutthroat world of business by accepting failure as a teaching opportunity, skillfully managing risk and uncertainty, and creating plans for dealing with rivalry and shifting market conditions. Entrepreneurs can convert obstacles into chances for development and success if they possess resiliency, persistence, and strategic foresight.

Chapter 7: Scaling and Growth

Increasing a company's ability to manage growth and growing its operations to access new markets, provide services to more clients, and increase earnings are all part of scaling a firm. Securing sustainable and profitable growth through scaling demands meticulous planning, intelligent decision-making, and efficient execution. We'll go over some of the most important tactics for developing and growing your company in this section, such as building out your business plan, strategically handling expansion, and boosting your personnel and infrastructure.

Expanding Your Business Model

To support development and expansion, broadening your product or service offerings, breaking into new markets, or looking into alternate revenue streams are all part of expanding your business model. The following tactics can help you grow your business model:

1. Product or Service Offerings Diversify: Find ways to expand your line of goods or services to better suit the changing demands and tastes of your target market. Introduce new product lines, variants, or expansions that appeal to various client categories and enhance your current offerings.

2. Enter New Markets: To reach unexplored markets and client groups, look into chances to expand into new geographic regions, demographics, or industry verticals. To find attractive prospects, evaluate market competition and demand, and create market entrance strategies specific to each target market, conduct market research.

3. Investigate Different Revenue Sources: Seek for creative methods to supplement your main business offers with new sources of income. If you want to increase profitability and generate new streams of recurring income, think about monetizing data and insights, licensing intellectual property, or providing subscription-based services.

4. Partner or Collaborate with Others: To take advantage of their networks, resources, and experience, form strategic partnerships or collaborations with distributors, suppliers, or enterprises that complement each other. Look into prospects for co-branding campaigns, joint ventures, or revenue-sharing agreements that will help you more effectively reach new markets and increase your reach.

5. Invest in Research and Development: Provide funds to support R&D initiatives in order to innovate and create new goods, services, or technology that meet the demands of developing markets or take advantage of market trends. Invest in state-of-the-art personnel, skills, and

technologies to propel future growth and maintain an advantage over competitors.

Strategic Growth Management

Setting specific objectives, giving projects top priority, and wisely allocating resources are all part of strategically managing growth in order to promote profitable and sustainable expansion. The following are some tactics for strategically managing growth:

1. Make definite objectives and benchmarks: Establish quantifiable benchmarks and targets that support your long-term vision and expansion aspirations. To guarantee accountability and alignment throughout

the organization, break down your goals into attainable targets and dates. Then, track your progress on a regular basis.

2. Prioritize Initiatives and Investments: Set priorities for initiatives and investments according to how they might affect strategic goals, profitability, and revenue growth. To optimize efficiency and effectiveness, concentrate on high-impact projects that yield the highest value and return on investment (ROI) in the shortest amount of time. Allocate resources accordingly.

3. Optimize Operations and procedures: To boost scalability, cut expenses, and enhance efficiency, streamline and optimize your company's operations and procedures. To increase productivity and performance,

pinpoint inefficiencies, bottlenecks, or areas that need improvement. Then, put solutions like automation, outsourcing, or reengineering into place.

4. Monitor and Manage Risks: Recognize and address possible risks and difficulties related to expansion, such as financial, operational, or market hazards. To reduce exposure and guarantee business continuity in the case of unanticipated setbacks or disruptions, create risk management strategies and backup plans.

5. Remain Adaptive and Agile: Remain adaptable and quick to react to shifts in the marketplace, consumer preferences, and level of competition. Be prepared to modify your priorities, strategies, or tactics in

response to changing market conditions or new possibilities and threats.

Scaling Your Team and Infrastructure

Increasing organizational capacity and capabilities to enable expansion and meet rising demand is the process of scaling your team and infrastructure. The following are some methods for growing your staff and infrastructure:

1. Recruit and Onboard Top people: Find and hire top people who will support your growth goals with their skills, experience, and cultural fit. Invest in training and development programs to nurture talent and promote career advancement, and

create strong recruitment and onboarding procedures to draw in and keep top performers.

2. Create an Expandable Organizational Framework: Create and put into place an organizational structure that will scale and grow with your company. Establish scalable procedures and workflows to facilitate cooperation, communication, and decision-making within the company. Clearly define roles, duties, and reporting lines.

3. Invest in technological and Systems: Make investments in scalable, effective, and innovative technological infrastructure and systems. To automate repetitive work, optimize operations, and facilitate remote

collaboration and flexibility, use scalable software solutions, cloud-based platforms, and digital tools.

4. Create Strategic Alliances: Collaborate with outside suppliers, distributors, or service providers to enhance your in-house resources and streamline processes. You can free up time to concentrate on key company priorities and strategic initiatives by outsourcing non-core services or processes to specialist partners who can provide knowledgeable assistance and cost-effective solutions.

5. Plan for Growth and Expansion: Make proactive plans to scale your team and infrastructure in anticipation of future growth and expansion requirements. To

anticipate future bottlenecks or limits and take proactive measures to solve them in order to support ongoing growth and success, develop growth projections, capacity plans, and scalability assessments.

You may set yourself up for sustainable and profitable expansion by growing your company model, strategically managing growth, and efficiently scaling your personnel and infrastructure. Through proactive and comprehensive scaling and expansion strategies, you may seize opportunities, surmount obstacles, and accomplish your long-term business goals.

Important turning points in the entrepreneurial path include scaling and growing. You may seize fresh possibilities, scale to new heights, and achieve long-term success in the cutthroat business world by broadening your company model, strategically controlling growth, and efficiently scaling your team and infrastructure. You may scale your company and achieve your goals of development and expansion by carefully planning, strategically executing your plan, and keeping an eye on long-term sustainability.

Chapter 8: Management and Leadership

Establishing and expanding a profitable company requires strong leadership and management. Leaders are essential in setting the company's course, encouraging and motivating staff, and spurring innovation and expansion. We'll cover important topics related to management and leadership in this part, such as creating a great workplace culture, managing teams effectively, and honing leadership abilities.

Developing Leadership Skills

For entrepreneurs to build confidence, encourage teamwork, and achieve achievements within their firms, they must possess strong leadership qualities. The following are some methods for enhancing leadership abilities:

1. Self-Awareness and Reflection: These are the foundational elements of effective leadership. Consider your areas of leadership strength, weakness, and room for improvement. Get input on your leadership style and its effect on others by asking colleagues, mentors, and staff members.

2. Continuous Learning and Growth: The path of leadership involves constant learning and development. Invest in chances for both professional and personal growth, such as conferences and workshops, executive coaching, and leadership training. To improve your leadership skills, keep up with developing leadership concepts, best practices, and industry trends.

3. Emotional Intelligence and Communication: To inspire and connect with people, cultivate emotional intelligence and good communication abilities. Actively listen, speak with clarity and empathy, and foster an environment of open communication and transparency within your company. Establish rapport and trust with your team by acting with genuineness,

empathy, and understanding in all of your interactions.

4. Strategic Vision and Thinking: Motivate people to support your business by clearly articulating your vision and strategy. Promote a feeling of direction and congruence by conveying the organization's overarching mission, principles, and objectives. To promote ongoing development and adaptation, reward your team members' creativity, innovation, and strategic thinking.

5. Empowerment and Delegation: Give your team members more power by granting them autonomy over decision-making, accountability, and authority. Give your staff the freedom and trust to own their

responsibilities and bring their special skills and viewpoints to the company. As needed, offer direction, assistance, and resources; but, refrain from micromanaging or stifling initiative and creativity.

Creating a Positive Company Culture

Attracting and keeping top talent, encouraging teamwork and creativity, and raising employee engagement and satisfaction all depend on having a positive company culture. The following are some methods for creating a positive workplace culture:

1. Explain Core Values and Beliefs: Clearly state and uphold the fundamental principles, values, and beliefs that shape your organization's identity and culture. Make sure your values and actions are in sync, and set an example by living them out in daily interactions and decision-making.

2. Promote Diversity and Inclusion: Create an environment where all workers feel appreciated, respected, and free to share their special skills and viewpoints. Establish a culture of belonging where people value one another's differences and see growth and opportunity as equals.

3. Promote Collaboration and Teamwork: Provide your organization with the means to foster cross-functional interaction,

collaboration, and teamwork. In order to accomplish shared goals and objectives, dismantle departmental silos and barriers and promote knowledge sharing, teamwork, and mutual support.

4. Recognize and Reward Excellence: Give staff members praise and awards for their accomplishments, contributions, and model conduct. In order to reinforce desired behaviors and outcomes, publicly recognize successes, milestones, and accomplishments and offer meaningful rewards, incentives, or recognition programs.

5. Promote Work-Life Balance and Well-Being: Give your workers' health and work-life balance top priority by providing flexible scheduling, wellness initiatives, and

encouraging policies and procedures. Establish a work environment where fulfillment, contentment, and health of employees are valued and encouraged both within and outside the office.

Effective Team Management

Collaborating with others, increasing productivity, and accomplishing organizational objectives all depend on effective team management. The following techniques can help you manage your team effectively:

1. Establish Specific Goals and Expectations: To guarantee alignment and clarity, clearly define expectations, goals, and objectives for

each member of your team and communicate them to them. To help your team members understand their roles, responsibilities, and performance expectations, give them direction, advice, and feedback.

2. Offer Support and Resources: Assist your team members by giving them the materials, equipment, and instruction required for them to be successful in their positions. Take down barriers, deal with issues, and offer direction and assistance when required to help them succeed and develop.

3. Promote Ownership and Accountability: Create an environment where team members accept accountability for their choices, actions, and results. Encouraging

your team members to take initiative, take charge, and be accountable means giving them the freedom to decide for themselves and work independently on problems within their areas of expertise.

4. Promote Collaboration and Communication: To develop a culture of teamwork and collaboration, encourage open communication, teamwork, and knowledge sharing among team members. To keep everyone informed and in sync with objectives and priorities, schedule frequent team meetings, brainstorming sessions, and project updates.

5. Give Feedback and Recognition: To support your team members' professional development, provide them with regular

feedback, coaching, and recognition. Give them constructive criticism for their work, acknowledge and celebrate their successes, and make an investment in their personal development by way of coaching, mentoring, or training courses.

Entrepreneurs can foster an environment where employees feel empowered, engaged, and inspired to produce their best work by cultivating leadership qualities, fostering a positive company culture, and managing teams effectively. A culture of trust, cooperation, and constant improvement can be fostered by entrepreneurs to create high-performing teams that propel success, growth, and innovation.

The fundamental pillars of organizational success are management and leadership. Strong leadership abilities, a positive company culture, and efficient team management are all tools that entrepreneurs can use to inspire, empower, and direct their organizations toward success and realization of their vision. Entrepreneurs can foster a vibrant organizational culture that promotes innovation, engagement, and long-term growth by putting an emphasis on communication, collaboration, and continuous improvement.

Chapter 9: Innovation and Adaptability

Being innovative and flexible are essential for any firm to succeed, especially in the competitive and quickly changing business environment of today. For entrepreneurs to succeed and keep a competitive edge, they must embrace innovation, be flexible and nimble, and react to market trends. We'll go into each of these topics in detail in this section and look at how innovators and adapters can be used by business owners to spur development and success.

Embracing Innovation

Entrepreneurship is rooted on innovation, which drives the development of new goods, services, and business models to satisfy changing consumer and market demands. Embracing innovation means fostering an environment in your company where experimentation, creativity, and constant improvement are valued. The following are some methods for welcoming innovation:

1. Create a Culture of Creativity: Promote innovation and creativity in your team members by fostering a collaborative and encouraging work atmosphere. Facilitate brainstorming, experimentation, and

discovery; additionally, recognize and honor creative solutions and endeavors.

2. Invest in Research and Development: Provide funds for R&D initiatives in order to stimulate creativity and the creation of new products. Invest in people, skills, and technology that will help you stay on the cutting edge of your field and predict and address new client demands and market trends.

3. Promote Experimentation and Risk-Taking: Encourage an environment where employees are encouraged to take risks and try new things without worrying about failing or facing consequences. Promote the idea that mistakes can be used as chances for development and progress.

4. Collaborate with External Partners: To gain access to fresh concepts, knowledge, and resources, work together with outside partners like suppliers, customers, colleges, or research centers. Create strategic alliances or collaborations that allow you to take advantage of networks, expertise, and resources from other sources to spur innovation and quicken expansion.

5. Remain Customer-Centric: Prioritize your innovation efforts by keeping your customers' wants and needs in mind. Get input from customers, pay attention to their views, and include them in the co-creation and development of new goods or services to make sure your innovations meet market needs and provide real value.

Staying Agile and Adaptable

Agility and flexibility are critical for overcoming uncertainty, grasping opportunities, and effectively responding to change in today's fast-paced and dynamic corporate world. Being proactive, adaptable, and resilient in the face of shifting market conditions and pressure from competitors is essential to remaining nimble and flexible. The following are some methods for remaining flexible and agile:

1. Embrace Change as a Constant: Develop an attitude that sees obstacles as chances for development and creativity and embraces change as a constant. Encourage your staff to pivot, iterate, and evolve in response to

changing circumstances by fostering an environment that is resilient and flexible.

2. Remain Adaptable and Flexible: Develop an adaptable organizational structure and decision-making procedures that let you react swiftly and forcefully to shifts in the marketplace or competitive environment. Simplify bureaucracy, provide frontline staff members the freedom to decide for themselves, and promote creativity and agility throughout the entire company.

3. Iterate and Experiment Continuously: Adopt an iterative process for problem-solving and making decisions by testing ideas, getting input, and modifying your plan of action in response to data and insights obtained in real time. Promote

experimentation and fast prototyping in order to swiftly validate concepts and gain knowledge from both triumphs and mistakes.

4. Adapt to Emerging technology: Keep up with trends and technology that could upend your business or open up new avenues for creativity and expansion. To stay competitive and future-proof your organization, invest in developing digital capabilities, utilizing data and analytics, and adopting emerging technologies like artificial intelligence, blockchain, or the Internet of Things.

5. Cultivate a Learning Culture: Encourage employees to learn new things and gain fresh perspectives in order to adapt to

changing market conditions and industry trends. This may be done by fostering a culture of continuous learning and growth within your company. To promote both professional and personal growth, offer chances for training, upskilling, and cross-functional collaboration.

Responding to Industry Trends

Staying ahead of the curve and taking advantage of new market opportunities require being receptive to industry trends. Through the observation of industry trends, analysis of market dynamics, and projection of future changes, entrepreneurs can strategically position their firms to achieve success and stay competitive. The following are some methods for reacting to market trends:

1. Observe Market Dynamics: Keep up with how your sector is affected by shifts in the competitive environment, consumer preferences, legal requirements, and technology improvements. To spot new trends and opportunities, keep an eye on rival activity, market research studies, and industry publications.

2. Anticipate Customer wants: By obtaining input from customers, carrying out market research, and examining consumer trends, you can anticipate changing customer wants, preferences, and behaviors. Keep an eye out for changes in customer behavior,

demography, and buying habits to spot untapped markets or product niches.

3. Remain Competitive: Evaluate your company's competitiveness by comparing it to competitors and peers in the same industry. This can help you pinpoint areas that need work. Examine the plans, offerings, costs, and marketing approaches of competitors to find any areas where distinction and innovation could be added or improved.

4. Innovate and Differentiate: Get ideas for innovation and difference from market research and industry trends. Determine the unmet wants, problems, or new trends in the market that could lead to the creation of new goods or services, or the creation of

new business models. To take advantage of market possibilities and keep one step ahead of the competition, innovate and iterate quickly.

5. Adapt and Pivot as Needed: Be ready to modify and reposition your operations, product roadmap, or company plan in reaction to shifting market dynamics or business trends. To be relevant and competitive, stay flexible and sensitive to changes in consumer demand, market forces, or outside influences on your company. You should also be prepared to make tactical changes as necessary.

In a business environment that is evolving quickly and becoming more competitive, entrepreneurs may position their companies for long-term success and sustainability by embracing innovation, remaining flexible and nimble, and reacting to industry trends. Entrepreneurs may stimulate creativity, build resilience, and take advantage of growth and expansion opportunities by cultivating a culture of experimentation, inventiveness, and ongoing learning.

In the quick-paced and ever-changing business world of today, innovation and flexibility are critical for fostering success and growth. Entrepreneurs may manage uncertainty, grab opportunities, and outperform the competition by embracing innovation, remaining flexible and nimble, and reacting early to market changes. By prioritizing inventiveness, adaptability, and ongoing enhancement, entrepreneurs can construct robust and future-ready enterprises that flourish in the face of alterations.

Chapter 10: Social responsibility and sustainability

Sustainability and social responsibility are becoming more and more crucial factors for companies of all kinds to take into account in the linked world of today. In order to generate long-term value, reduce their influence on the environment, and advance social justice, entrepreneurs must integrate sustainable practices, give back to the community, and strike a balance between profit and purpose. We'll go into each of these topics in detail in this part and look at how business owners may incorporate social responsibility and sustainability into their operations.

Incorporating Sustainable Practices

Adopting socially and ecologically conscious company practices that reduce adverse environmental effects, preserve natural resources, and advance social justice and inclusiveness are all part of incorporating sustainable practices. The following are some methods for implementing sustainable practices in your company:

1. Reduce, Reuse, Recycle: To reduce trash generation and encourage resource conservation, put recycling and waste reduction initiatives into place. Minimize

the use of non-recyclable and single-use plastics, and whenever feasible, give preference to reusable or biodegradable substitutes.

2. Energy Efficiency: Investing in energy-efficient appliances, lighting fixtures, and technology can increase energy efficiency and lower greenhouse gas emissions. Reduce energy use and your carbon footprint by putting in energy-saving devices like programmable thermostats, LED lighting, and solar panels.

3. Sustainable Sourcing: Purchase products, ingredients, and raw materials from ethical and sustainable vendors who follow environmental laws, fair labor standards, and responsible sourcing procedures. Give

preference to vendors who assist local communities, reduce waste, and use renewable resources.

4. Carbon Offsetting: Invest in carbon offset programs like reforestation, renewable energy, or energy efficiency initiatives to balance carbon emissions from travel, business operations, and logistics. To lessen your influence on the environment, join forces with respectable carbon offset companies or buy verified carbon offset certificates.

5. Life Cycle Assessment: Examine the environmental impact of your goods and services from birth to death by conducting a lifecycle assessment. To reduce environmental impact and improve

sustainability, find ways to optimize product design, manufacturing procedures, packaging, and distribution networks.

Giving Back to the Community

A crucial component of corporate social responsibility is giving back to the community, which enables companies to improve society, assist local communities, and advance social welfare and development. Here are a few methods business owners may support their community:

1. Corporate Philanthropy: Contribute a part of your earnings, goods, or services to nonprofits, charity groups, or neighborhood

projects that share your goals and beliefs. Make a significant impact on other people's lives by supporting causes that pertain to social justice, healthcare, education, the environment, and poverty alleviation.

2. Volunteerism and Employee Engagement: Promote employee engagement in the community and volunteerism by providing paid time off, putting together group volunteer initiatives, or matching staff contributions to nonprofit organizations. To promote a culture of giving back, involve staff members in fundraising campaigns, community service projects, or mentorship initiatives.

3. Skills-Based Volunteering: Provide pro bono services or use your business

knowledge, abilities, and resources to assist nonprofits or social entrepreneurs. Provide technical support, capacity-building assistance, or strategic consultation to help organizations fulfill their objectives and make the most impact.

4. Community Partnerships: To address urgent social concerns and work together on community development projects, form strategic alliances with nearby nonprofits, educational institutions, governmental bodies, or community organizations. To address common problems and develop long-lasting solutions, combine resources, exchange knowledge, and make use of networks.

5. Environmental Stewardship: To save and conserve natural resources and wildlife habitats, take part in environmental stewardship projects like tree planting, habitat restoration, beach clean-ups, or environmental education campaigns. To advance sustainability and environmental awareness, collaborate with environmental organizations or take part in neighborhood-based conservation initiatives.

Balancing Profit with Purpose

Pursuing both financial and societal objectives at the same time as well as incorporating social and environmental factors into corporate decision-making processes are necessary to achieve "profit with purpose." Entrepreneurs can generate shared value for stakeholders and support sustainable development by coordinating their corporate goals with more general social and environmental goals. Here are some methods for striking a balance between purpose and profit:

1. Triple Bottom Line: Adopt a triple bottom line strategy that takes into account social and environmental effects in addition to financial performance. In order to generate sustainable value for society and shareholders, measure performance in terms of people, planet, and profit. Strive to optimize outcomes across all three dimensions.

2. Business Models Driven by Mission: Create a mission-driven business model that centers your operations and commercial strategy around social or environmental impact. Establish a distinct goal, mission, or social cause that is in line with your beliefs and appeals to your target market. Then, utilize this goal as a benchmark to direct resource allocation and decision-making.

3. Impact Investing: Look into options for social entrepreneurship or impact investing that produce both financial profits and favorable social or environmental effects. Invest in or lend support to companies, startups, or projects that, while generating sustainable financial performance, solve social or environmental issues like access to

affordable housing, renewable energy, or healthcare.

4. Corporate Governance and Transparency: To guarantee responsibility and moral conduct, adopt sound corporate governance procedures and transparency in reporting. To establish confidence and trust, communicate with investors, clients, and communities and share social and environmental performance metrics, goals, and activities.

5. Long-Term Value Creation: Prioritize sustainable growth and long-term value creation over maximizing short-term profits. Prioritize investments and activities that bring about long-lasting constructive change and advance the greater good, and

take into account the wider effects of company actions on society, the environment, and future generations.

Through the integration of sustainable practices, community outreach, and a purpose-driven profit margin, entrepreneurs may create companies that not only generate profits but also have a positive effect on the environment and society. A more just, resilient, and sustainable future may be built for everybody by entrepreneurs who embrace sustainability and social responsibility as fundamental values and guiding principles.

In order to generate value for stakeholders, reduce their influence on the environment, and advance social welfare, entrepreneurs must embrace sustainability and social responsibility as essential components of contemporary business practices. Incorporating sustainable practices, contributing to the society, and striking a balance between profit and purpose can help entrepreneurs create companies that are not only profitable but also socially and environmentally conscious. Future generations can benefit from sustainable growth driven by entrepreneurs who prioritize producing shared value and beneficial societal impact.

Chapter 11: Reflections and Lessons Learned

Thinking back on one's entrepreneurial journey is a useful practice that provides insights into one's own development, accomplishments, setbacks, and lessons discovered. People can obtain insightful knowledge and wisdom that can guide their future ventures and encourage others to follow their own entrepreneurial route through personal experiences of success and failure, important lessons learned from the entrepreneurial journey, and guidance for budding entrepreneurs.

Personal Stories of Success and Failure

Each entrepreneur's path is distinct, filled with both successes and failures that mold their experiences and results. An intimate look into the highs and lows of business is provided by personal tales of success and failure, which can inspire and educate others.

Although difficulties, setbacks, and periods of uncertainty are common for entrepreneurs, how they handle these situations ultimately determines their level of success. Aspiring entrepreneurs who may be starting their own entrepreneurial journeys might benefit from the inspiration, motivation, and perspective that come from hearing human experiences of overcoming adversity, seizing chances, and reaching milestones.

Success stories highlight accomplishments like starting a profitable business, scaling operations, creating a beneficial influence in the community, and demonstrating the benefits of hard effort, persistence, and creativity. These narratives honor the spirit of entrepreneurship and provide motivation for those who wish to follow their passions and bring their ideas to life.

On the other hand, failure stories offer insightful perspectives on the difficulties and dangers of being an entrepreneur, highlighting errors, blunders, and setbacks that occur during the journey. While failure is an unavoidable aspect of the entrepreneurial path, it can also be a tremendous teacher, providing insights on growth, resilience, and flexibility. Entrepreneurs may de-stigmatize setbacks, normalize the learning process, and inspire others to accept failure as a necessary step on the path to success by sharing their stories of failure.

Key Takeaways from Entrepreneurial Journey

Thinking back on the entrepreneurial path provides insightful information and important lessons that can influence strategic direction, direct personal and professional development, and educate future decision-making. Entrepreneurs frequently extract wisdom from their experiences, turning lessons into useful knowledge that they can share with others and use for their own gain. Several important lessons learned via the entrepreneurial path include:

1. Resilience and Persistence: In the face of difficulties, disappointments, and uncertainty, entrepreneurship demands resilience and persistence. People who learn from their mistakes, stay optimistic, and endure through hardships are frequently the ones who achieve success.

2. Adaptability and Flexibility: Success as an entrepreneur depends on your capacity to adjust to shifting conditions, change course when needed, and welcome innovation.

Entrepreneurs that are flexible can take advantage of opportunities, negotiate the intricacies of the industry, and stay ahead of the curve.

3. Risk-Taking and Courage: Venturing outside of one's comfort zone and taking risks are fundamental to entrepreneurship. Innovation and growth require the guts to embrace uncertainty, take measured risks, and go after big ideas.

4. Focus and Discipline: Achieving goals and objectives in the business path requires maintaining discipline, focus, and prioritization. Success requires avoiding distractions, adhering to one's goal, and efficiently allocating time and resources.

5. Continuous Learning and Growth: The path of an entrepreneur is one of ongoing learning and development, with chances for advancement and enhancement presented by every encounter. Long-term success requires adopting a growth attitude, asking for feedback, and making investments in both professional and personal development.

Advice for Aspiring Entrepreneurs

Aspiring business owners who are just starting out frequently ask successful business owners for advice and direction based on their own experiences and observations. This guidance is based on personal experience and insight gathered by enduring the highs and lows of being an entrepreneur. Common recommendations for would-be business owners include the following:

1. Follow Your Passion: Make endeavors consistent with your interests, values, and passions. Selecting initiatives that excite you and align with your fundamental values is an important step in the road of becoming an entrepreneur.

2. Embrace Failure: Accept failure as a necessary component of the entrepreneurial path and as a chance for development and education. See failures as instructive experiences that offer perceptions, criticism, and chances for development.

3. Build a Strong Network: Embrace the opportunity to surround oneself with a network of peers, mentors, advisors, and collaborators who can provide perspective, support, and advice. Through networking, you can have access to priceless tools, chances, and contacts that can hasten your entrepreneurial path.

4. Remain Resilient and Persistent: Develop resiliency, perseverance, and resolve in the face of difficulties, disappointments, and impediments. To succeed, maintain your concentration on your objectives, your ability to adjust to change, and your will to endure hardship.

5. Never Stop Learning: Make a commitment to lifetime learning and

ongoing development by looking for chances to increase your level of knowledge, proficiency, and competence. Accept fresh experiences, difficulties, and development chances to advance as a leader and business owner.

6. Stay True to Your Vision: As you travel the entrepreneurial path, hold fast to your vision, values, and mission. Stay true to who you are and what you're here to accomplish, trust your gut, and follow your intuition.

It is possible to motivate, educate, and inspire people to follow their entrepreneurial dreams and make a positive, long-lasting impact on the world by reflecting on personal stories of success and failure, summarizing important lessons learned from the entrepreneurial journey, and providing guidance for aspiring entrepreneurs.

Writing about one's own experiences with success and failure, summarizing important lessons learned, and advising prospective business owners are all beneficial activities that support learning, inspiration, and personal development.

Entrepreneurs who reflect on their experiences are able to share their wisdom with others, recognize trends and lessons learnt, and obtain important insights into their journey. By means of contemplation, entrepreneurs have the ability to motivate, instruct, and enable the subsequent cohort of prospective entrepreneurs, cultivating a climate of inventiveness, adaptability, and influence within the entrepreneurial community.

Conclusion

Embracing the Entrepreneurial Spirit

As our investigation into the world of entrepreneurship draws to an end, it is evident that adopting an entrepreneurial mindset involves more than just launching and expanding a company; rather, it involves a way of life, a mentality, and a path of both professional and personal development. People experience obstacles, disappointments, victories, and changes during this trip that mold their goals, values, and personalities. We'll consider the essence of the entrepreneurial spirit, honor the achievements of entrepreneurs, and encourage readers to realize their own entrepreneurial potential in this last section.

The Spirit of Entrepreneurship at Its Core

The entrepreneurial spirit is fundamentally made up of inventiveness, perseverance, ingenuity, and resolve. It is the motivation behind those who have the guts to dream big, take calculated chances, and devote themselves wholeheartedly to their hobbies.

Curiosity, flexibility, and a never-ending quest for perfection are the hallmarks of the entrepreneurial spirit, which drives a never-ending cycle of expansion, exploration, and discovery. Entrepreneurs are trailblazers who forge new routes in unexplored regions, visionaries who spot opportunities where others see barriers, and change agents who upend the current quo and expand the realm of potential.

Remembering Achievements in Entrepreneurship

Building businesses and earning a profit are only two aspects of entrepreneurship; other goals include leaving a lasting legacy and having a meaningful effect. Entrepreneurs are change agents who propel economic growth, innovation, and the creation of jobs in local communities all over the world. Through their projects, services, and products, they enhance lives, solve urgent problems, and bring innovative ideas to life. Every type of entrepreneur, from little startups to large multinational companies, leaves a lasting impression on society, culture, and advancement.

Inspiring Readers to Embrace Their Own Potential as Entrepreneurs

I encourage readers to think about their own entrepreneurial potential and the opportunities that may arise as we draw to a close on our adventure into the world of entrepreneurship. Adopting an entrepreneurial mindset can lead to countless opportunities and possibilities, regardless of your experience level or if you're thinking about starting your own business. It's about having the guts to go for your goals, the fortitude to get over setbacks, and the vision to build a better future for both you and other people.

To change the world, embrace your passions, use your creativity, and reach your full potential. Every journey starts with a single step, whether you're starting a new business, pursuing a passion project, or starting a new job.

Dare to dream large, have faith in your abilities, and have faith in yourself. As you travel, assemble a network of peers, mentors, and advisers who will be there to guide, encourage, and inspire you.

Recall that failure is a necessary step toward success as you traverse the highs and lows of the entrepreneurial journey. Accept failures as teaching moments, change course when called for, and never stray from your goals and principles.

As you develop, change, and invent further, remember to remain inquisitive, insatiable, and modest. Above all, keep your entrepreneurial spirit fueled by your passion and purpose at all times.

In summary, cultivating an entrepreneurial mentality involves more than just starting firms; it involves adopting a curious, creative, and resilient way of thinking that enables people to follow their passions, add value, and have a positive influence on the world. In honoring the successes of businesspeople and encouraging others to realize their own potential, let's not forget that the path to success in entrepreneurship is a journey full of chances for personal development, fulfillment, and exploration.

In summary, adopting an entrepreneurial attitude and way of life allows people to follow their passions, add value, and have a good influence on the world. It goes beyond simply launching and expanding a firm.

Let us keep in mind that the entrepreneurial journey is a journey of personal and professional growth, full of opportunities for learning, innovation, and transformation, as we consider the essence of the entrepreneurial spirit, celebrate the successes of entrepreneurs, and encourage others to embrace their own entrepreneurial potential.

www.ingramcontent.com/pod-product-compliance
Lightning Source LLC
Chambersburg PA
CBHW060051260726
48658CB00004B/1262